NEGOTIATING
WITH YOURSELF

women making midlife
career changes

FORLAGET SØERNE // SOERNE PUBLISHING

MALENE RIX

NEGOTIATING
WITH YOURSELF

women making midlife
career changes

NEGOTIATING WITH YOURSELF
Women making midlife career changes

Publisher: Forlaget Søerne, Copenhagen, Denmark
Print: Books on Demand GmbH, Norderstedt, Germany

Copyright Malene Rix
First edition 2019

Cover design: www.workofheart.com
ISBN 978-87-996592-3-4

CONTENTS

Foreword	07
Introduction	13
Part One: "The real me...right now?"	23
1 Something is not as it should be	24
2 Saying no	29
3 Choosing yourself	32
4 Worn-out strengths & hidden talents	37
Part Two: "What motivates me?"	44
4 Stuck	45
5 Self Determination Theory	49
6 Basic Need: Autonomy	51
– having a say	
7 Basic Need: Competence	55
– using meaningful skills and abilities	
8 Basic Need: Relatedness	58
– feeling like an accepted part of a community	
Part Three: "What to do?"	63
9 The current status	64
10 Same but different	69
11 Testing, testing	72
12 Negotiating with others	76
12 Negotiation Techniques	80
Afterword	90

FOREWORD

"What would you really like to be doing?" Irene glances at me, then turns her head and gazes out of the window. We are sitting in a small office with a view of the harbour waterfront in Copenhagen, trying to discover a way forward for her in her work life. Then, with a big smile, she says, "I would love to import and sell food from the region I come from in Spain". Her whole face lights up and the deep frown she had on her face, when she first started talking about the problems she faced at her current work place, disappears. Instead she starts to describe her ideas, and she laughs when I tell her about the amazing transformation in her face, her expression, her whole body, that I can see. She came to talk with me about salary negotiations in her current job but instead we explored her dream of starting her own business.

Taking the leap
This scenario is fairly typical when I talk to people and we explore their work-life negotiations. We always start with thinking about what really matters to them now, as individuals. The difference that I see in someone's expression when they are talking about what they would love to be doing, rather than what they should be doing, is startling and revealing. Following our conversation, Irene decided to quit her job. She found a small shop, from where she now sells delicious Spanish food and organises parties and events with her food as the main ingredient. Sounds easy? Deceptively so, and yet Irene's journey was and is not without its problems. That first meeting gave her the small push that she needed to set her on the new path for

which she had craved at a deeper level. Together we explored how she could do this, instead of getting stuck with why it was a bad idea. The drive and energy generated by an idea already grounded within her boosted her efforts and she never regretted taking the leap. The more we believe in what we ask for and convince ourselves that it is the right thing for us, the easier it is to look and sound convincing to others. The process of discovery injects the energy and stamina that will propel us forwards.

My work
For more than twenty years, I have worked within the field of negotiation, both as trainer and advisor to people of all ages, from all walks of life and from different countries and cultures. Our conversations about negotiation have often become very personal ones, as we end up talking about each individual's negotiation with themselves. The surprised look and then the wry smile I frequently see, when I mention how often we have to negotiate with ourselves, is why I have decided to write about this fascinating part of the negotiation process. We sort of know we do this and also often realise, that the negotiations we have with ourselves can be a real challenge. As I am a middle-aged woman, talking to many other women at this life-stage, the focus on women and their thoughts on career change as a very typical negotiation with yourself, seemed a natural one, although the messages are relevant for all. I would like to thank all the people who have shared their stories and examples with me over the years, and the amazing team who have helped me to make this book.

This book
If and when you decide to look more deeply and think about your working life and what, if anything, needs to change, I hope these pages will inspire you. The need for a pit-stop, and a chance to re-

assess and even change direction, often crops up in mid-life, when we are well and truly established in our work or far enough along to get a glimpse of what life after work might look like. I suggest you ask yourself three questions: Firstly, Who is the real me…right now? _ to reflect on who you are with all that you know and can do. Secondly, What motivates me? – to check all batteries and understand what drives you. And finally, What will I do about it? – to find out which practical tools to use on your way forward.

Women's stories
I have chosen to use examples mostly from women in this book, but anyone can read it and draw something from the experiences described. Gender is a critical issue when we talk about negotiation, and particularly in the negotiations we have with ourselves as preparation for negotiating with others. More often than not I hear women who are almost too concerned with what others might think about a possible change. This is not because they are poor negotiators. It is to do with our expectations within society of how 'selfish' women are allowed to be. Is it ok to put yourself first, before any needs that your family might have? This question, and the tendency for women to tick all boxes before looking for a new job or way to work, will have a significant impact on how and if you choose to make a serious change in your work life.

Expecting a negative response
When we, as women, take care to consider those around us and their needs, it can be a very wise thing to do. If we decide to negotiate our way to a change that affects others, it's good to make sure that they are all on board. However, if we worry too much about what others might think or say, it can have a negative backlash, particularly if we anticipate resistance. Women will generally be judged differently

from men when they are asking for something or are ambitious for themselves. If we suspect that our wish to make a change will be met by the response, 'But what about me, then?' – we may tone down our own ambition in our desire to accommodate the needs of others.

Smart moves
The best way to give ourselves the gentle push that we all need when we might face possible resistance in a change negotiation, is to be well prepared. And the first step is our negotiation with ourselves, before we navigate the process of engaging others. We do not need to think like an alpha male or force ourselves to step up in ways that are not comfortable. But it is important for our inner motivation and drive, to use all the techniques and advice available to us to ensure that we achieve what we set out to do. This will also enable us to shatter some of those unhelpful gender stereotypes that we may encounter along the way.

What if...
If we choose to change career and the way we work, this is hopefully about a change for the better. The more people, men as well as women, who visibly refuse to follow the typical career paths staked out by history and tradition, the more others will be inspired to take alternative paths that lead to a more meaningful working life. There is currently a strong imbalance in power and influence in society that needs to be addressed. However, the best way for women to shift the balance may not be to claw our way into a world of round-the-clock work that leaves very little room for anything else – unless, of course, this is a way of life one genuinely enjoys. It has become a truism that in order to get somewhere in your career, you must work like mad – there are no free lunches. What if the women who dare to say no to an outdated model for organising both life and work, were

at the forefront of a new wave of alternative working? This would demonstrate what someone can achieve without spending all her waking hours at work. What would it mean if instead we made serious attempts to change the way power and influence is parceled out, both politically and structurally?

Something to think about
This book is full of questions – many rhetorical questions but also quite a few for your own use. At the end of each section of the book, there will be a list of questions to work with. Read them and choose the ones, you find most interesting to think about, talk to someone else about or write notes on. Throughout the book there will also be some exercises to try out, but the questions and exercises are not meant as a manual to work through, and then you will come out the other end with the perfect game plan. Thinking about making a big change in your work life is not a linear process, and I find that working on the questions you find most intriguing at a certain point in time might be just as helpful. So, jump in wherever you like, and I hope that simply by taking time to consider these questions will get you rolling.

Other books
I am inspired by a number of writers and researchers whose work adds insights to this often lengthy, highly individual and sometimes bumpy process. This book is designed to be the hand on your back and the gentle push that will encourage you to read more widely. At the end of the book, you will find a list of recommended literature with a short review that outlines why this might be useful to you.

INTRODUCTION

Negotiating with ourselves
Throughout our lives, we negotiate with ourselves, consciously or unconsciously, about our jobs and careers. We make decisions about whether to move or stay put, to go for a promotion or even to change direction completely. A negotiation starts the moment there is more than one option or possible solution in a given situation. Deciding what to choose, where to go, what to aim for will have to be discussed and the options weighed up, before we can agree on the best of these options. This process usually includes an element of disagreement within ourselves, which may not always be serious or insurmountable. However, sometimes the obstacles in our heads are so big that the solution is not obvious.

The voices in our heads
A debate takes place inside our heads when we try to decide what to do for ourselves. Some people talk about the devil on one shoulder and the angel on the other, both locked in a battle for their attention. But mostly it's a straightforward negotiation with ourselves and the various wishes and desires inside us. I want to stress that this is a negotiation, because it may take some creative thinking, some give and some take, in order to reach a decision that we are happy with. In constructive negotiation, it's not about only one option being 'right'. It's about trying to marry the various options and finding a way to address all the concerns and desires that we have.

So, in your mind, try to imagine your negotiation with yourself as a group of people sitting around a table, each with their own opinion about where you should go. Now you have a starting point from where you can listen and examine each voice. Where do the voices come from? They may belong to others in your life who are important to you, or they may represent your own ideas of who you are, what you are good at or where you should be at this particular moment in time. Your job is to listen and to find creative solutions to the big question: Where do I go from here?

Midlife make-overs
Once the hectic decades of building a career and perhaps starting a family are over, it is not unusual to come up for air, to make space for or be forced by circumstances to take a birds-eye view of our working lives. This is when many of us feel the need to give our lives a serious make-over. A good starting point for this is the statement: 'I want the rest of my working-life to be the very best!' However, to align what we do and how we work with the opportunities of middle age, involves far more than a quiet reflection over a cup of coffee on a Sunday morning for most of us. In our 40s, 50s or 60s, with a good chunk of our lives still left to play with, we are in a stronger position to make wiser career choices than we were starting out. By now, we have a clearer idea of what we like to do, who we are as people, how to do things. So, it ought to be easy sitting down with a pen and paper to create the perfect mid-life career change plan, right?

Kids, cars and houses
One problem is that along the way we have become tethered to our own world, to important people and places, to lovely houses and comfortable cars, to gardens that need tending or dogs that need walking. And we all have a many-layered story that describes who we are as working people, which for many of us will be an important part of our identity. So, changing our career, or even our profession, may seem like a huge challenge as it is likely to involve a change in how

we see ourselves as well as how others perceive us. As if this was not enough of a challenge, other factors play an important role as well.

Women change midlife
Dealing with radical change when we are 'midlife' is inevitable, particularly for women. Menopause and its many consequences, both physical and emotional, brings its challenges. Physical symptoms may throw us off track. A well-known TV-presenter recently talked about how disruptive she found hot flushes in the middle of an important interview. Who would take her seriously when sweat was pouring down her face? Menopause can also affect our mood. Some women say they feel more angry and impatient, others describe themselves as overly anxious and weighed down by constant rumination. However, once women understand how much these physical changes affect them, that they are not alone in this, and that there are things they can do to help themselves, then the pressure often lifts and some aspects become easier to handle. Talking to others about this change, that one gynecologist described as by far the biggest physical change in a woman's life, can be a really important part of understanding our current state of mind.

Psychological barriers to change
Not only do we face physical, and possibly emotionally disruptive, change midlife, certain psychological barriers can also hold us back. A friend told me how she had serious doubts about leaving her full-time career at the age of 33. Her concern was a fear of suffering a loss of status and not having a clear answer when asked what she did for a living. We often confirm our social status through conversations with others about jobs and careers, so leaving a secure job can produce a range of reactions from incredulity to embarrassment. What is left to talk about, then? My friend started doubting whether

she had anything to contribute, and a fear of failure loomed large in her mind. These thoughts and misgivings rarely diminish with age. Many women I meet tell me that, once they hit 45, they become more aware of the knowledge that applying for jobs post-50 can be a real challenge. Taking a leap into an unknown career at that age can feel risky.

Changing roles
Society's perception of middle-aged women and their role also greatly influences our own thoughts about ourselves at this crucial time of our lives. Many women say they feel 'invisible' to others once their childbearing days are over and struggle with this. One friend told me about her need to 'keep up' physically with younger women in her workplace, and to stay attractive to men. As an influential public figure and CEO, she was convinced that her power would diminish when she became less physically attractive and was no longer able to flirt as part of 'the game'. For some women, rethinking what and how they work will be affected by this perspective. It will influence how they think about their changing role and society's perceptions of them. It will also provide the freedom to choose. I have heard many women describe this new phase in their lives in positive terms, once they have come to terms with the change – a sense of relief arising from a different kind of attention and respect, which is both satisfying and empowering.

Scarcity – a lack of time and money can make it difficult to change
Serious adjustments to our working lives will require courage, energy and the time to think careful thoughts; plus money, of course. We may have wanted to find other things to occupy our waking hours for many years but never had the time to give this proper attention.

If/as our time becomes easier to manage, we may start to think about the risk to our personal finances of a major change. Worries about having enough time and/or money will, at the same time, reduce the bandwidth of our minds. This can make it difficult to escape a situation of scarcity. There is no easy answer to how we can find the money or the time to enable us to jump into an unknown future. I'm fully aware that many women are locked in this dilemma with little wriggle-room. However, I would still like to encourage you to reflect on the kind of changes you would like for yourself, as a first step to a different future.

Creating room to manoeuvre
Several people that I have talked with, set up a separate 'enough-is-enough' account which has helped provide them with the catalyst and courage to change their working lives. One woman describes this money as her safeguard against having to stay in an unhappy work situation; a savings pot means she can evaluate a job with an open mind and the freedom of choice to walk away. Another told me how lack of time in a busy work life held her back from thinking clearly about her job situation and explained how she eventually decided to take three-weeks unpaid leave. She spent this time in her basement with flipcharts and coloured pencils, to generate thoughts and ideas about her next step. Those three weeks were hard-earned; she struggled to keep the needs of her family and the rest of the world at bay, but she succeeded and made a rough plan for her next move.

Small experiments
With even the smallest window in our lives, we can experiment. We can try out different prototypes or ideas of our new and improved working life without placing everything on the line. We read about people selling their homes, investing all their money in a great idea

for a new app, and making many millions – high profile success stories that we hear most about. However, there will be many examples of people creating important and lasting change for themselves who decide to start small and try different options before they are able to articulate their final destination. A friend of mine had always loved taking photos but never saw it as a way of living. As she started taking more formal portraits of people, the very enthusiastic feedback she received made her venture out and apply for a few professional photography jobs. Today she takes photos, makes videos, designs websites and advises people on social media. Over the years, she has gradually built her business and slowly relinquished her former day job.

Respecting others' concerns

When making serious changes in our lives, negotiating with ourselves is complicated at the best of times. If our minds are preoccupied with daily demands on our time and money, then the whole process will be affected. At the same time if we, ourselves, are concerned about the consequences of changing, it is likely that the people around us will be too. They will not necessarily share our inner urge or our belief in how much good the change will bring. They may express concerns about how our change will affect them and what it will mean for their lives – about the implications of a possible failure, which may be irreversible. Hearing others' sometimes sceptical remarks and seeing their resistance in this light can sometimes make it easier to deal with. Instead of becoming angry or despondent, we need to listen hard to discover the source of their concerns, as the first step to find our way around the negative reaction.

The best question of all time

When negotiating with our different selves, and with all the people around us, the most important task is to ask ourselves the following question: What will it take for me to be able to say yes? The key to progress lies in facing up to each of the potential barriers to investigate what it would mean if we were able to move beyond these obstacles. Ask yourself the question What will it take to start this process of change? Ignore the nagging inner voice that's questioning whether you should make a change at all or which is urging you to let sleeping dogs lie. By asking yourself the incisive question, What will it take to start this process of change? it will help you to deconstruct the obstacles and find creative ways around them. I find this helps particularly when our concern for others' needs and wants threaten to make us give up all together.

Bite-sized investigation
There will always be many objections and rational explanations for why our ideas for change are unrealistic and off the table. Chopping these obstacles into bite-size pieces may make it easier to look at the *how*, rather than becoming stuck in a negative spiral. Indeed, the question What will it take?, may produce some answers that make the project seem initially impossible. "In order to do this, I would have to win the lottery" or "We would need to move but my partner will never agree to live in another city". However, if we ask ourselves What will it take? to go deeper, the chances are that we will find inspiration and even solutions for how best to proceed: 'So, I need money… what will it take for me to get my hands on some?" or 'What will it take for my partner to agree to moving? What would they miss and how can we work around this?'

Digging deep
When I talk to people about their negotiations with themselves, we touch on many issues, some of which may be very personal and deep-rooted. Together we have to explore the layers of good and bad

experiences, wishful thinking, real and imagined obstacles, old habits and stubborn perceptions that people hold about themselves. At those moments, I am looking for the light that I saw in Irene's eyes, the energy and enormous drive that people are sometimes able to tap into, if they delve deeply enough to find the source in response to the larger question: What do I really want to do with the rest of my working life?

QUESTIONS TO ASK YOURSELF
Choose the ones you find relevant

// What made you pick up this book?

// What is the current status of your work life?

// What ideas or hopes for the future make you want a career change?

// What circumstances can't be changed, but need to be worked around?

// What circumstances can be changed, if you work on them?

// What will make it OK to put your needs before that of important others' needs?

// If negotiating with yourself involves hearing the 'voices' of those around you which will influence your change – who are these people? And what are they saying? Do some of them need replacing?

// What will your surroundings gain, if you make a change for the better?

// What would your family/friends/colleagues miss, and how can you work around this?

// What will happen, if you don't do anything at all?

// What will it take to start this process of change?

// Who can help you?

PART ONE

The real me...right now?

SOMETHING IS NOT AS IT SHOULD BE

Tina had spent over twenty years working as a journalist within corporate communications in a large technology company, happily going with the flow and moving up and around in an organisation that grew and expanded over the years. Whenever there were major changes, she found a new job within the company until her focus had changed from corporate communications to a more strategic advisory role: "The job became more about strategy and how to spin a story and I was never very good at this – I didn't like it." She felt increasingly uncomfortable with the work she was expected to do and one day had the realisation that she had become a less pleasant version of herself:

"I found myself constantly muttering negative, almost disloyal things in corners. I became a really horrible person to be with. I believe that one has to be a decent person, I have to, my colleagues have to and our bosses too. If this is not how people are made to behave in an organisation – myself included – I feel a huge resistance inside and I have to take this seriously; otherwise I end up reacting in really inappropriate ways because I'm so very frustrated with the situation."

This was not easy to admit and act upon but when she saw herself from the outside and was able to pinpoint where all the frustration and anger came from, this acted as a catalyst for Tina. Her first step was to create distance and do some soul searching, so she decided to leave her job. She then negotiated a deal with the company in which they fired her and agreed a severance package. Tina was then able to take time out and think about what her next step should be.

Pivotal moments
These pivotal moments are always part of the stories I hear about

people making serious changes to their work life. It is often a specific event such as a new boss, being fired, a divorce, the experience of serious illness or the loss of someone close that jolts us out of our daily routine. We then look in the mirror and really see ourselves. The need for change can also sneak up and manifest itself in unspectacular ways: a sinking feeling waiting for a train on a Monday morning or the sudden realisation that we have spent hours on social media whilst at work over the past week. We rarely have the time or energy to monitor if we are still on track and true to our dream of a great career – life gets in the way. We get comfortable, we are both relieved and flattered to be offered a job and a salary and with this comes ease and sometimes complacency. We do not feel the urge to rock the boat. This may be a good place to be. However, even if the path we end up taking feels relevant at the time, if the underlying values and purpose of the work are not true to who we are, then a roadblock may appear and force us to stop and think again.

Saying yes to something better
When we realise that something is not as it should be, it can provide the shock that kicks us into action. This awareness may start slowly, as a quiet whisper, 'this is just not okay, I don't want to live like this.' However, it may soon become a strong and outspoken no! The decision not to carry on with the status quo has to come from a deep conviction - that to say no to what doesn't work is our first step in saying a confident yes to something better.

A pebble in the shoe
As a midwife, Jeannette worked for five years in the public health sector before she realised that conditions there made it difficult for her to do the job to the standard she thought was right. After a few attempts to work within the profession but in an alternative way,

Jeannette decided to pursue a career in leadership, another great interest of hers. She enrolled on leadership training and, after a number of job changes, is now head of a department in a large technology company, a completely new direction and sector for her. Jeannette's process of change has been interesting. She struggled for some time to make her actual job as a midwife align with her deeply-held values about how to best help the women she worked with. A strong sense of dissatisfaction with how the profession of midwifery had developed felt like a pebble in her shoe that she kept trying to adjust. Although Jeannette tried out a number of different approaches to her work in midwifery, her frustrations finally made her leave the field.

Leaving the tribe
When Jeannette talks about this transition she says:

"When I explain why I left midwifery I tend to choose one of the many reasons that best fits the conversation. Some people are able to hear all the difficult things I had to deal with when I worked as a midwife, like unfit parents or children who suffer illnesses, and listen to all the times when things don't go well. With others, I simply tell them that I wanted to spend more time with my family and sometimes I just say that the cutbacks in the national health sector are the main reason for quitting."

Midwives have a distinct identity and one that most of us would associate with a genuine calling. This makes it particularly difficult to change tack and leave. It is a credit to Jeannette that as a grounded and robust person she has coped well with leaving the community. When describing a situation where a woman decides to stop working in midwifery, it is not unusual for a colleague to say that she was 'never a good midwife' or that she 'didn't fit in'. This illustrates how difficult it can be to pursue a new direction, particularly if this is a radical departure. Leaving behind one truth about who we are in our work, to explore a different side of ourselves, can be daunting.

Older and wiser
It can be a serious business to deconstruct what we do and how we live in order to explore alternative avenues. However, finding the courage to break something down will often make room for new and exciting horizons. As human beings, we have a strong instinct that tells us when we are right about the world. We can then learn to develop healthy doubts about what we see and know. A step into the unknown is bound to involve bad decisions – we think we have it all worked out only to find that the reality is not as we thought. Allowing ourselves to be wrong and being open to this along the way is important. This is where I believe that we dare to fail a bit more as we become older and wiser. The older we get, the more we realise how unpredictable the world is and how impossible it is to control. It becomes easier to shrug and say "Oh well, let's try something else, then."

Challenging questions
We may wake up suddenly one morning and realise that instead of working in the health sector we should, perhaps, have been a biodynamic farmer. Or we might discover that the way we talk about our current work has become wearingly negative. Either way, to know that we must respond to this new awareness will force us out of our comfort zones. Change is daunting for most people: innocent questions from well-meaning friends, 'So what do you want to do, then?' or 'Who are you really?' can derail us. The uncertainty that follows can make us feel like a construction site inside with wrecking balls flying about, creating chaos and driving dust into our eyes. Old ideas about who we are and what we do no longer seem to ring true. Many

people describe this process as terrifying and certainly not positive. However, in spite of this, a more radical demolition of old structures may be exactly what we need as a first step towards genuine transformation.

SAYING NO

Elizabeth worked in the pharmaceutical business as a highly specialised consultant for many years. Initially she was employed in a large international company but when she was fired, she had to rethink and look for other work. As an experienced and competent person, Elizabeth was keen to make the right next move. At first, she tried out a number of jobs within the same field that didn't last very long. Once she had discovered that a new job was not a good match, she made a quick decision to move on and look further afield. In a certain way, she used her negative experiences to help her navigate. She became aware that a particular kind of work environment and boss made her respond badly, "In my last job I sat in front of a computer and was told which key to punch. I hated it. And my boss was quite incompetent. He made some completely wrong strategic choices and expected me to applaud him for that. I just couldn't do it and when I feel like that there is no hiding my frustration - I become a real pain to be with." It may sound like a negative guiding principle, but I find that many I talk to could use a bit of Elizabeth's ability to quickly identify that something is not as it should be, and then act upon it.

Finding the strength to object
When we reach a certain age, it is easy to feel impatient with meaningless work or incompetent bosses. Luckily, with age, we also develop our conviction that it's okay to say no. One of the images I use in my negotiation training sessions is that of a tree. The roots of the tree represent what we as people really believe in, what is important to us, our values and deeply held beliefs. These are all the things in life that we say yes to. The trunk of the tree represents where we stand firm, where we say no. And finally, the top of the tree represents all the alternatives that will move us forward together in a negotiation, al-

lowing us to cultivate something new instead. The image is from The Power of a Positive No by William Ury, one of the founders of constructive negotiation. The key message in the book is that if we find it hard to say no to something or someone, we need to have a good look at the roots of our tree – the yes behind our desire to say no.

The yes behind the no
When it is hard to say no, it is closely connected to a fear of negative consequences. It is both relevant and valuable to consider how the other person will react to your no to their request, to think about the impact it may have on the other. However, instead of letting the negative predictions stand alone, it helps to also imagine all the good that will come of your saying no. It could be the need to say no to a job that includes weekend work or which takes us away from home four-nights a week. By saying no to these conditions, we are saying yes to more time with our family and friends. We are also saying yes to the time we need to pursue our other interests and to get enough sleep and rest to do our work properly.

I think to myself:
"I really need to spend time with my family at weekends without having to think about work. Everyone suffers if I have to miss out on this (YES!)"

I say to my boss:
"I'm afraid I can't work this Saturday, (NO) but I am happy to see if we can reorganise things to get the work done throughout the week? Involving some of the people from the other department? Postponing other tasks? (YES?)"

The yes? that follows the no
So, instead of preparing a lot of arguments and explanations for

your no, it's much more helpful to think of if and how you can help the other person find a solution anyway. Replacing "No, because…." with "No, but what about…." will move the conversation forward in a more constructive direction, and you won't have to defend or justify yourself to the same extent. What you are in effect doing, is negotiating your way out of the situation. Thus, the wrapping of the no in two yeses, will help us to negotiate with ourselves at times when we fear the consequences of giving a negative response.

Moving on from the no
Whilst it is important to say no when we don't want to do something anymore, the follow-up question of "Let's find out what we both can say yes to instead" is just as vital. Sometimes we are pushed and pressured and the no response comes naturally. However, if no is all we can say then we are depending on someone else offering a new way forward and suggesting new possibilities. If we sit back and wait for a change to come to us, all we can do is to cross our fingers and hope that the right things will fall into our lap. To say no to what doesn't work for us in our careers is a vital first step – and finding out what we would like to say yes to is the next logical stage.

CHOOSING YOURSELF

In recent years, it has become popular for people to look for the 'best version of themselves'. Although it may be a positive to look inside ourselves for what we like best, the notion of finding a best version of who we are risks denying the many other versions of ourselves that exist, both good and bad. In essence, I don't believe that we all have a perfect inner-me waiting to be revealed. Yet I do think that to deepen our understanding of what is valuable and important to us at a particular time is an important and continuous task. Our choice to explore what is meaningful to us, right here right now, is more open-ended than looking for and finding the best version of ourselves. If we believe that the process of the task is in itself useful, this will help to facilitate our more active and meaningful engagement in this.

My sister, the doctor
I have always been envious of my older sister who knew from a very young age that she wanted to be a doctor. She chose the right path for her, even though it has been challenging at times. However, even though she found her core work identity at an early age, I have watched her experiment and develop how she works: doing research, deciding to change her field of expertise, becoming a senior consultant and, more recently, taking time to teach and participate in political work. So even when we are clear about our choice of profession, the decision to adjust the framework in which our work takes place can be a powerful one – it can help us to find the optimal conditions to achieve our best. Instead of calling it the 'best version of myself', I prefer to call it the best version of a working life for me, and this we can all influence greatly. My sister recently told me that she now feels at the very top of her career – she has finally found a position

that suits her perfectly and where her age and experience give her the power and influence to do what she likes most.

A continuous process

Our perception of self is deeply affected by the many roles we have in life and the relationships and communities we are a part of. As circumstances change, and we become older and wiser, things happen to us. At this point we need to adjust and look for, or even write, our own story. We need to look back, with kind eyes, on who we have been and what we have done and accept this as our story. It also means grabbing a pen and deciding to write the next lines ourselves – to make it our own story instead of letting others write it for us. When we choose ourselves in this way, we also take responsibility for who we are. This is a fundamental job for us all, every day, as we live and experience the world alongside other people. It is not a quest to find our one and only true self. Rather it is a continuous negotiation, a choice about who we are, what we want to do and how we want to be with others. This conversation changes all the time - it is continuous.

Upwards and onwards

Suzanne worked hard as head of communications in a large financial institution, flying around the world, working late and also at weekends. She told me her best friend described her as '…always running' - to and from meetings, to pick up kids, to meet friends and so on. This comment hit her hard and became an image of how wrong this job had been for her. For many months, she had thought seriously about changing her job when one day, just as she was facing a large audience of employees at a conference, she reached a conclusion - a clear thought came into her head; "I just shouldn't be doing this. It's not who I am." She told me she had felt completely empty inside and guilty that she couldn't deliver what people expected of her. Her position at work had developed over time, in an upward direction and also further and further away from Suzanne's core interests. She had lost touch with who she really considered herself to be professionally, and in spite of having been promoted and appreciated in her work, she could no longer ignore that she was way off track. Suzanne resigned and took some time out to think and to try to find out who she really was and wanted to be at this point in her life.

Fundamental values
Many of the stories I hear when people tell me about making important changes for themselves depict a discovery, or a rediscovery, of certain important fundamental values they have. Like Tina, the journalist whose career path was determined by her company; "The job became so strategic that it all felt like a lot of spin, I didn't like it. All this strategic sugarcoating of a lot of nonsense... the staff saw right through it and laughed. To me it felt like a lack of respect for the employees." She could tolerate the situation no more and longed to get back to doing work that actually meant something and was in tune with her values – to help people. So, as we grow older and have learned a thing or two about ourselves, our most fundamental beliefs will become clearer. These building-blocks emerge when the top layers of our lives are scraped off. As we uncover these, they become the foundation of the new working life we are creating.

Many different identities
We have many identities and our work identity is one of the most prominent. Jeannette, the midwife turned leader, is an example of someone who always knew that she had several different interests and possible professional selves. For her it was not difficult to imagine a different career. Nevertheless, some people identify so much with their work that leaving it would mean leaving a part of them-

selves behind. This can make a change of career that has been forced all the more traumatic. Whatever the circumstances, a change in direction will mean that we need to write the next story of who we are. This is all the more reason to find the core values that will motivate us to change or that will help us to move on to something new. Jeanette left her sector because she really wanted to do a good job made difficult by a health system dealing with cut-backs and rationalisation. Her core values were compromised and she was quick to recognise this and react. She was also lucky enough to have alternative interests and angles to pursue.

Working identity
Prof. Herminia Ibarra from INSEAD is an expert on transitions. In her book, Working Identity, she shares several interesting thoughts about how we all have multiple working identities. One of her central points is that we carry around a 'whole cast of characters, the selves we hope to become, think we should become, or even fear becoming in the future.' (p38). Discovering these selves and allowing ourselves time to flow back and forth between these different versions of who we were, are, and would like to be, is crucial to achieving necessary insights about which identity suits us best. Prof. Ibarra illustrates how these periods of transition are almost always painful; we struggle to let go of the old and embrace the new. Taking time and experimenting will help us discover the way ahead.

Being a good parent
In many of my conversations with women in particular, the need to change is also connected to the desire to become a better parent. This is in itself a strong pull and the expectations of the world around us play an important part here. Hannah, who worked for many years as an executive in the financial sector, chose to become an independent

consultant because she wanted to become more flexible and to spend more time with her children,

"Being able to stop work early and pick up my kids and then spend the afternoon with them was really fantastic! I went back to work in the evening when they were asleep and worked sometimes until 2 am – but that was fine. I felt good being able to tick the 'great mum' box, and nobody could criticise me for being a bad parent. Some people had hinted at this when I worked full-time and travelled a lot – they questioned my choice from that perspective."

Some might suggest that Hannah should ignore societal pressure to pursue her full-time career. However, if you have both a strong career drive and simultaneously wish to spend time with your children, then looking for ways to accommodate both needs can motivate you to change. Not giving up on one of these things but finding a way of achieving both.

Conflicting identities
Women who choose a career are still being challenged by what others may perceive as conflicting identities; How to combine being a good mother with spending so much time at work? I often hear how much this affects the choices they make. This identity conflict will often be a strong factor when women choose to go out on a limb and make a serious change. For many it will add an extra layer of positive energy, which will stimulate them to find a new way of organising their working lives. The trick for them is to ensure that they don't lose their preferred professional identity along the way. It involves weighing things up. For some it is an incentive to start a new career that will encompass both their need to believe in themselves as a good parent, and their desire to have a great and fulfilling job.

WORN-OUT STRENGTHS & HIDDEN TALENTS

Some years ago, I attended a workshop on strengths with an inspiring psychologist Dr. Robert Biswas-Diener. Before the workshop, we completed an online test, in order to uncover our strengths – all of them. The test differentiated between realised and unrealised strengths. It also revealed our learned behaviours; the things we have become good at but don't really enjoy that much. My younger sister took part in the workshop and we spent an interesting weekend uncovering the strengths we enjoy using the most, the strengths that give us a push and the energy to move forward. Having my sister there was a huge bonus - someone who I could talk this through with who knew me well. When we looked at the test and particularly the unrealised strengths, she was able to confirm some of the things I didn't see in myself and give me examples of where she had seen me use these strengths. It was a huge confidence boost and made me want to explore the whole spectrum of my strengths.

No more Ms. Nice Guy
My sister and I have often reminded each other of the workshop and how we must reduce the tasks and jobs where we use our learned strengths, the things we are good at but don't really enjoy doing. It has become obvious to us both how difficult it can be to break free from doing work that others – and sometimes ourselves – think we are good at, even when we know that this work is draining us of energy. I once met a Norwegian woman, an architect, who had moved to another country with her husband and five children. She was unhappy with her then situation as an unemployed professional and as a more than full-time mum. One of her comments struck me. She told me that she received a lot of positive feedback from her husband and family who said what a great parent she was and so amazing

to cope with five young children. This feedback was nice to hear, of course, but what she longed for more than anything was to be recognised and appreciated as a professional architect. She was a highly competent parent but she needed to use her full range of strengths to be really happy.

Too responsible
When we talk about their working lives, women often tell me that they are tired of being 'too responsible'; experienced enough to analyse and predict how things will pan out in a given situation at work, and obliged to make sure that everything runs smoothly. We may be good at something but it doesn't mean that we enjoy doing it. Yet if we are both responsible and capable, it is hard to ignore disasters looming, especially if we know how to prevent them. Christine, a friend who works part-time for a church organisation, described how she answered e-mails from her sick-bed so as to manage her projects even when running a high fever and feeling miserable. All of a sudden it struck her - her boss would get the impression that she couldn't be very ill as she continued to work, which made her attempt at being 'responsible' even more obviously futile.

When sacrifices go unnoticed
Doing all the daily work that keeps everything and everyone on track can be thankless task. When we take on more of the jobs that we may be good at but no longer enjoy, at some stage, this will no longer be enough. Like Christine, who worked whilst running a high fever, the sacrifice we make may go unnoticed and more often than not, remains unappreciated. This leaves us with work we take no pleasure from and get no acknowledgement for. So, when we start to feel that the bulk of what we do is something that just needs getting over with before we can get to the fun stuff, then perhaps it's time to stop and

have a closer look at our many strengths. Taking part in a workshop is one way of exploring this, but some relatively simple thought experiments and small exercises will also get you a long-way.

The wind in your sails
An image that Dr. Biswas-Diener shared with us, and which I often think about, is of a yacht taking in water as a picture of how it can feel to be unhappy about something. We can spend too much time trying to find and fix a hole in the hull of the boat – talking over the obvious problem and trying to understand what has caused it. But fixing the hole won't make the ship move forward. We also need to look at what constitutes the wind in our sails, what gives us the energy and propulsion that we need. Finding out which of our core strengths we genuinely enjoy using will supply that very same gentle breeze. When we are clear about which parts of our working life motivate and give us energy, and about those elements that drain our personal resources, this will provide us with some important clues.

Exercise:
A simple exercise is to tell someone your plans for the week at work. Meetings scheduled, reports to hand in, customers to see, books to balance – try to be as detailed as you can and remember all those things you actually do, not just the ones you are meant to do. Before you start, ask the person listening to watch closely for the moment that your face lights up. It may be a slight change but it will be there, I promise. Let them make a note of this and share this with you afterwards. You can also simply record yourself on camera and have a close look afterwards – there will no doubt be some things you enjoy doing more than others. Ask yourself, When does my face light up? and Why do I think this is?

Women under pressure

I work as a volunteer counsellor with women who now live in Denmark who have chosen to move here from other countries. Many of these women struggle to find a job here. They say it is hard to become integrated into society and often they have heavy family responsibilities. We talk about job-hunting and how difficult it for some of them to have the education and professional experience they bring with them acknowledged, mainly because they don't speak Danish. Many of them end up taking any kind of job to make ends meet, and this often means doing work that is a long way from what they trained to do and from what really interests them. When they bring their most pressing problems to our conversations these commence on a heavy note. They do indeed look like captains on a sinking ship. So first we look at what constitutes the leak in their boat, and then I concentrate on helping them to find the wind in their sails.

Core strengths

When they come into the room, it is often with a deep frown and very serious eyes. Then we start to discover what they really enjoy, what a perfect job for them would be – and slowly we move beyond their self-limiting assumptions – away from what they feel they should do or have been doing for some time. Eventually we reach the part where they allow themselves to dream and to imagine they are doing what they really enjoy. The physical change is remarkable. I see a spark in their eyes, they smile and may even laugh and suddenly we have a lot more things to work with: core strengths that give them energy, new ideas and possible scenarios. Some of these may be crazy and wild but all of their dreams contain vital information and inspiration in them. Translating these into a job is not always easy. However, this information and their new energy are essential ingredients that will assist them to move on.

Hidden talents

Maria, a thirty-something Polish woman, was struggling to find relevant work in the environmental sector. With a university degree, she had spent a number of years in Denmark working as an administrative assistant in a small NGO. Her frustration was primarily that the job she had didn't enable her to make use of her specialist knowledge and her short-term contract was ending. She expressed a sense of hopelessness, a lack of confidence in her own worth and value, and a deep pessimism. We spent time digging as deeply as we could to find out which of her abilities she most wanted to use, and discovered along the way that she had some additional skills that she would like to activate. One of these was her ability to network, to engage with people and access their knowledge. Just looking at her face when she described how much she enjoyed meeting other people said it all. We had a closer look at her job-situation and found ample opportunity for her to network in the right environment, to use her natural curiosity and flair for talking to people and, with these skills, to discover new work possibilities for herself. Knowing that she had the ability to do more of what she was good at boosted Maria's energy considerably.

Exercise:

Choose a time or a specific job or task where you felt that you made a real and positive difference. Tell another person about this and ask the listener to help you to reveal which of your strengths and abilities this story demonstrates. Ask them to listen for what the story says about you and what you are good at. It may involve a few false starts but it's always good to talk positively about yourself and to listen to someone's story with a specific investigation in mind. For example, as the speaker someone may tell a story about making a great sale to a happy customer, and perhaps the person listening also hears that the speaker has a talent for collaborating with back office colleagues, which will help to see the sale through. They may hear that the speaker is a creative person, who is determined to find the right solution for their client even if this takes time. As a result, the speaker can add 'patience' and 'persistence' to their personal list of strengths, along with the ability to work well with people from different parts of the organisation, to achieve shared goals.

This exercise is inspired by the late Dr. Peter Lang from the Kensington Consultation Centre

QUESTIONS TO ASK YOURSELF
Choose the ones you find relevant

// What is not as it should be in your work life?

// Is there a 'no' you would like to say to something/someone?

// What would the positive consequences of your 'no' be for you? And for others? Immediately and/or long-term?

// What other options are there, that will help you move forward and still say 'no'?

// What were your hopes and dreams when you first started working?

// Getting the bigger picture: Draw a straight line. Start from the left and fill in your career developments, placing the jobs/positions you most enjoyed above the line, and those you haven't liked below. What are your thoughts when you look at this map?

// Think of the times you have felt most happy and proud of your work. What was your identity then? Describe the person others would see in you.

// What would you say your core values are? Are you able to live by your values today?

// Ask someone who knows you well when was the last time you told them something positive about your work. Dig around and find out what they saw and heard? What does this tell you?

// Make a list of all the things you do at work. All of it. Perhaps even things you have done in previous jobs. Then go through the list and evaluate each task according to the following questions:

> Am I good at this?

> Do I enjoy doing this? Or not?

> Does this work give me energy? Or does it drain me?

> Which of your strengths and abilities would you most like to use in the future?

PART TWO

What motivates me?

STUCK

When I was in my mid-thirties, I had an interesting conversation with a close friend about my work. At the time, I was living abroad and working in communication and project management for an international organisation, which on paper had seemed the ideal job for me. But I felt completely stuck. I wasn't using any of the skills I most enjoyed. Every time I suggested a change or a new initiative my boss politely but firmly told me no because it would rock the boat and create unnecessary and unwelcome attention. My colleagues were nice but we each sat in our own offices in front of a computer, and only saw each other for lunch. There were no joint projects or interesting collaborations – we were just quietly clicking away at our desks. However, I was earning a decent salary. I had friendly colleagues and a very light workload. I worked for a respected organisation, had peace and quiet and could feel secure in my position – what was not to like? What shocked me then was how doing nothing and feeling completely sidetracked simply ground me down and left me miserable. My skills and competencies were not in demand, my initiatives were ignored and there was almost no collaboration with anyone – some of the most fundamental motivational factors were simply not there and it made me unhappy.

Accessing important experiences
Having listened long enough to my moaning, my friend started to ask me in detail about what part of my working life so far had made most sense to me. During this conversation, I remembered a course I had done in negotiation technique some years earlier as part of a job as a producer and project-leader. During this training-course I had discovered all the brilliant uses of negotiation and had felt inspired. I realised that I used negotiation, unconsciously, as a life skill.

My parents had, unknowingly, brought us up to negotiate our way through obstacles rather than 'fight or flee'. The basis of all constructive negotiation appealed to me – both in a practical sense and also as a more gentle and pragmatic way to solve differences and respect other people's views and wishes, without having to concede my own.

Seeing the light
To me it was a revelation that negotiation could be a way to help and accommodate others and their viewpoints and, at the same time, to protect my own ideas and have my own way as much as possible. All of this could be achieved without having to confront endless conflicts or through heated debates. I had never been very good at arguing but didn't see an alternative way to deal with disagreement. So, my discovery of straightforward negotiation tools came as a huge relief and was accompanied by a great feeling of joy. The consultants teaching the course had noticed my enthusiasm and also spotted that this energy might be turned into business. After the course was over, they approached me to hear if I would be interested in working for them as a trainer.

Stumbling on gold
I wasn't able to accept the offer at the time so I didn't pay much attention to it. However, during the conversation with my friend, I remembered it and it felt like someone had pushed me in a new and exciting direction and, most importantly, now I held a compass in my hand. The training course I did originally was not part of an attempt to widen my career options or improve my CV. I had simply felt the need to sharpen this skill and I stumbled on something that would eventually become a meaningful career path for me. Once I decided to make a serious change and try to pursue this new path, I felt both a push away from my current job and a strong pull towards a poten-

tial new career. Even so, the change wasn't easy. It involved moving country and rethinking the framework of my private life. Nevertheless, once I had started down this path, there was no going back. I had found a really valuable source of energy based on pure interest and internal motivation.

SELF-DETERMINATION THEORY

Motivation is a huge topic but it is an essential one when we talk about negotiating with ourselves. There are many approaches and much has been said in the field of motivational psychology but one theory in particular has made a lot of sense to me, both personally and professionally. Self-determination Theory (SDT) first came to prominence in a seminal work by Edward L. Deci and Richard M. Ryan published in 1985. Deci and Ryan were interested in finding out what motivates people to do things just for the sake of doing them, without any external reward or other factors outside ourselves. Being intrinsically motivated means we are propelled forward by an energy that comes from within – in essence, SDT explains that if we as human beings are prevented from doing what we are intrinsically motivated to do, it will spell trouble.

Three psychological needs
Deci and Ryan found three universal, psychological needs that are key to our wellbeing and that form the basis of intrinsic motivation: Autonomy; to feel you have a say in your own life, Competence; to experience mastery and being acknowledged for this, and finally Relatedness; to be connected to and care for others. These basic internal needs are like a lens through which to look at people who are not satisfied or feel out of balance. It is likely that their state of mind may be connected to these three needs being unfulfilled. As a negotiator, being conscious of these needs at all times is how I manage to communicate and facilitate the negotiation process. They are also pointers to keep in mind when we make agreements – to be mindful about how to meet these needs in our fellow negotiators. As a consequence, everyone will be happier with the result and more motivated to follow through.

The needs as a guide

When we make changes, or want to find a new direction in our careers mid-life, then what drives most people to that place is the need to honour these intrinsic needs more carefully than we did when we were younger. We are motivated by many things and typically, when we are younger, there are strong, extrinsic motivators at stake. Earning money, being able to establish ourselves physically and professionally in the world and perhaps supporting a young family are some of the key factors. Once we hit middle age, many people I speak to discover that material things mean less and less compared to the importance of doing something worthwhile with their time. When I talk to someone about why they want to change direction, I hear strong echoes of these motivators – that people have discovered or rediscovered these intrinsic needs which have become impossible to ignore. So, used as 'filters' to evaluate our current job situation these three needs act as inspiration for where to go from here.

BASIC NEED: AUTONOMY
– having a say

Sometimes people understand autonomy as being independent, alone and free from others. However, in this context, the meaning is a little different. Autonomy has much more to do with the ability to influence your own life and decisions about what to do and how. Many years ago, I had a wonderful boss who always gave me a choice when I came to him with a problem. He said, "What do you need from me? I can take the problem away from you and fix it; I can tell you what to do right now; or I can listen to you telling me what you think might be a good way to solve this?" Not surprisingly, nine out of ten times I chose the last option because I really was the person who knew most about the problem and I wanted to fix this for myself. He could have just said, "Fix it yourself – you can do it" but then perhaps I would have thought that he didn't care and had left me hanging. Or his response might have been; "I'll deal with it" leaving me to wait and hope he did the right thing. He gave me options, and encouraged me to work it out for myself and, as a consequence, I had a great sense of achievement once I had solved the problem. The really clever thing was, of course, that he didn't end up adding yet another thing to the pile of issues to resolve on his own desk.

Time to change...again
When I decided to join the negotiation consultancy as a trainer all those years ago, it was a really happy move and I spent a few years developing training concepts and learning how to teach. My colleagues were amazing and my boss was the best. But soon the small company merged with a larger one and the feeling of being part of a joint endeavour faded, as did the possibility to work in those areas we all felt most motivated by. The parent company had other ideas and

suddenly the framework for my job started to disintegrate; valued colleagues resigned, projects changed into something I didn't enjoy doing and management styles clashed with my core values. Eventually I decided to leave and become an independent consultant.

Buckling up
Going solo and starting my own business had never been part of my plan and I was scared and extremely nervous about the prospect of not having a steady income or a solid framework around me. However, after a few crucial conversations with good people – who helped me to analyse the worst possible scenarios and think of a few alternative routes in case of total failure – I was able to strap on my parachute, buckle up my belt and get ready to jump. When I finally jumped, I discovered that, instead of feeling as if I was free floating over a giant chasm, I was still standing. I felt as though I had made a small hop, equivalent to moving from the pavement into the road. What I had imagined as a huge change in my life turned out to be an adjustment for the better. I could now work with the content and the competencies I most enjoyed and was good at, without the restrictions of an organisation that was moving in the wrong direction for me.

Freedom to choose
I had the opportunity to decide so many things for myself: the direction of my work; who to collaborate with; and where to explore new areas of interest. This has been the biggest and most positive experience in my career. My work is now tailor-made to suit my interests, my competencies and my values. It has been a genuine eye-opener and I am truly happy in my work. Bills have to be paid so I can't always choose freely what to do and who to work with, and the world doesn't always want to buy what I would most like to sell. However, the fundamental feeling of being in charge of my career and having

the possibility to freely craft the content of my work, is hugely satisfying. I have had my share of hopeless bosses and am now old and wise enough to have something to offer the world. As a result, I feel highly motivated, particularly by the freedom to choose what I think is best for me.

Independent – not alone
Many people who work independently tell me how much they treasure this freedom. They value the choice to do what is right in their own view and not to be deflected by the decisions of others, particularly if they consider these to be the wrong ones. As we get older, we are less tolerant of fools, so the need to have a say in what we do, and how, grows with time and experience. One independent consultant told me that when she decided to look for a job again, the headhunters said that having had her own business was not an advantage. Initially she was surprised until she heard that many companies are worried that someone who has made their own decisions will be hard to manage. I subscribe to an alternative perspective, which is that companies should be deeply grateful to find employees who understand the need to get at job done. If you have been independent, you know you have to deliver the goods sometimes outside conventional hours. The concern, of course, is that people with a strong sense of autonomy are unlikely to take orders and execute them blindly. They will need good leadership which, unfortunately, is in woefully short supply in many work places.

The instinctive path
Caroline is a designer, who has moved into corporate HR. She designs and facilitates development processes for managers. She describes her experience of working with a senior manager to put together a two-day event for his colleagues:

"He let me take charge. Not of the content itself but I was able to influence design and facilitate the process. He trusted me enough to let me do it my way, which was by no means the usual approach. I'm sure he kept a close watch but he let me have extremely valuable time – 25 of his top people for two days – and it went really well! This experience was very important in finding my true calling: to help people navigate in chaos. This is the basis of the consultancy that I am now setting up."

Caroline told me that when she has a particular job to do, she tries to find the route which is most straightforward and instinctive for her. In this way, she is able to use the skills and abilities which come most naturally. This has had consequences – she has had to change jobs a couple of times, for example. For Caroline however, autonomy within her job really matters and without undue compromise, she has made steady and incremental progress in her career.

Drive
In his book Drive!, Daniel Pink shares a number of real-life examples of how companies that focus more on what people do, rather than how many hours they spend at work, tend to be more successful. By limiting the amount of day-to-day control, an employee's sense of autonomy will increase. In these circumstances, each employee is invited to make an active choice about how to approach his or her job. So, autonomy is not about going solo but about having the freedom to decide important things for ourselves – which then motivate us intrinsically. This also makes business sense. Particularly later in life, when external rewards have less significance and we know more about ourselves, many people seek to make changes in the pattern of their working lives that will enable this fundamental need for autonomy to be met.

BASIC NEED: COMPETENCE
– using meaningful skills and abilities

Elizabeth, the highly specialised consultant from the pharmaceutical industry I talked about earlier, is a clear example of how important it can be to use your skills and abilities and to get proper recognition for these. Elizabeth is an expert in getting new types of medicine validated. She has the type of knowledge that can make a huge difference to many people. In her old job, she partnered up with the inventor of a new drug and, together, they had an exciting time developing the drug. Slowly the politics of the organisation and the administrative demands took over, and Elizabeth ended up with such serious stress symptoms that her doctor ordered her to go home immediately. She told me; "I simply couldn't take it anymore. I was sick of having to nod and agree and never getting the chance to discuss things. I just wanted to use my expertise and work for the end purpose: to get important drugs approved so they could start to help people."

Using your competencies in the right way
Like Tina, who became so far removed from using her core skills as a journalist that she couldn't recognise herself; or Jeanette, the midwife, who felt like a cheat when she had to justify the cutbacks in the service to expectant women, we have an intrinsic need to work with something we know we are good at. This is at the very core of so many of the conversations I have with people who wish to change career direction. Jeanette was so unhappy working in the national health sector that she tried to set up her own private clinic to give women the treatment and care she knew worked best. This was also in an attempt to apply her own knowledge to the full. In the end this didn't work out for Jeannette. However, it shows the lengths to which she was prepared to go to use her capabilities in the right way. Jean-

nette told me that, statistically, almost 50% of trained midwives leave the field after five years. In 2016, for example, the UK Royal College of Midwives published a report that revealed three main reasons why midwives were exiting the profession in such numbers: staffing levels and workload were two key factors. However, the quality of care that they were able to give was the third contributor - not being able to do what's best for the women in their care and finding it hard to live with that, just like Jeannette.

The value of doing competent work
When I discuss the possibility of starting up a new business with a client, I always look for clues that will help them to identify which of their competencies they would most like to sell. Being an independent operator may be wonderfully boss-free. However, to drive both work and career ourselves, to put a value on what we do and then sell this to others, demands a huge amount of energy. At this point, our intrinsic motivation will be vital. If we decide to do something that we enjoy, for its own sake, then we have access to a wealth of energy and enthusiasm. This not only helps in the day-to-day challenge of driving a business forward, it also makes us more persuasive and convincing as professionals. Working with negotiation makes sense to me on so many levels and the feedback I often get from course participants is that they can see I believe in what I'm teaching. This doesn't mean they all buy my message but they do respect my authenticity.

Integrated lives
A colleague once told me, that the whole discussion about work-life balance didn't make much sense to him. He was an extremely busy CEO of a huge cultural institution and he always looked relaxed and happy when we met, even when describing serious challenges

in his organisation. His comment came in response to my incredulous, "How do you manage?" He explained that since he enjoyed what he did, the sharp division between work and free time, or 'life', was not really relevant for him. This was not to say that round the clock working was his whole life – but it explained that, as he was in a position to work with his core interests and strengths, many of the things he did at work he would have enjoyed doing anyway. Being successful at what he did had much to do with the satisfaction he took from this and the belief that he made a difference. You may think that it's all very well when you're the CEO and in charge but his work was highly determined by a large number of stakeholder interests, both internal and external. His comment has stayed with me as it provides a clear picture of how much energy and strength can be found if we are in a position to do work that we are truly interested in and for which we have a talent.

BASIC NEED: RELATEDNESS
– feeling like an accepted part of a community

Remember Hannah, who went from being an executive in the financial world to become an independent consultant? After she had worked independently for many years, she decided to go back into a large organisation. Hannah had missed the feeling of connection and the opportunity to celebrate success and progress with colleagues and co-workers. She said; "I still wanted to do the same type of work and also to share success with other colleagues. I had missed this when I was working on my own; but before, my need to be autonomous was obviously stronger for me." Hannah actually laughed when she then told me, 'I still behave as if I were my own boss at times, thinking that it's a human right to decide for myself when and how to do my job!' Luckily her present employers are wise enough to see that Hannah is at her most productive when she is allowed to work in the way that she prefers.

Missing the team
It often strikes me that when I read about job satisfaction, and what makes us happy at work, that people usually score the category 'my colleagues' high-up on the range of motivators. The opportunity to share success and offer support to each other when times are tough is something most people value immensely. A colleague from my time as a consultant also jumped ship and became an independent trainer in her field. This was not in response to an urgent need to be her own boss but more to escape an untenable work situation. At that stage, she had no clarity about what else she might do. Over the years, she has found it a continuous challenge to not be part of a team, to have no boss, and to find herself alone with the, sometimes difficult, tasks of selling her business, delivering services and client debriefing. She

is a highly intelligent person and very sociable. She enjoys the process of bouncing off ideas, talking things through and being encouraged by others – this is a key motivator for her. For her, the solution was to find partners and other small businesses to join-up with and to realise that she misses the crucial energy that comes from collaborating with others and being a team-member.

Extend your horizons
When I think of my life as an independent consultant over the years, the need for connectedness has been very important. Fortunately, I have had very good clients for many years and some of the people with whom I work on joint projects are also long-time colleagues. Then again, like Hannah, I can miss the joy of celebrating a job well done with other people. Being aware of this intrinsic need continually drives me to find projects that have this element. More recently I have started to look more broadly – at my work and all the things I do as part of my business and on a voluntary basis and at how I develop my ideas and interact with the world – like writing this book, for example. I have found that certain corners of my business call for me to take part of study groups or voluntary projects, where there is a great sense of community and connection. So, we can expand the sources that satisfy our basic need to belong, so this embraces many areas of life, including spare time activities, family and friends, and voluntary work.

Psychological needs as a framework
The three psychological needs of Autonomy, Competence and Relatedness provide a helpful lens through which to scan and monitor our working lives. To be alert to opportunities and to seek out activities that we enjoy for their own sake and then to analyse what, how and who makes these activities enjoyable, makes good sense. In

my own experience, this constant attention to what motivates me helps when I negotiate with myself about the direction that I might take. These motivators become an overall framework through which to review my activities as they help me understand what I need to do, and with whom.

QUESTIONS TO ASK YOURSELF
Choose the ones you find relevant

// What is your main motivation for doing the work you do? Money? Recognition? Making a difference to someone? Have a think about whether you are motivated by external (extrinsic) things or if your motivation comes from within?

// Look back at your career and see if you can identify moments of being intrinsically motivated, when you have felt energy and enthusiasm about what you did. What were those? How did it feel to be motivated from within?

// Have you become more or less focused on being intrinsically motivated with age?

// Do you have enough of a say in the work you do now? Regarding the content, who you work with, the practical framework for doing your job?

// What would it take for you to have greater influence on what, how or with whom you work?

// Which of your talents would you most like to be recognised for? To what extent does that happen already?

// What would a job look like, where you could focus on your core interests and strengths?

// What do you most enjoy about working with others? Both formally re. the content and informally re. the social interactions?

// When and how do you feel most connected to others at work? What makes this possible?

PART THREE

What to do?

THE CURRENT STATUS

What is your current state?
Some years ago, I taught a leadership course with a brilliant colleague, who was a successful leader in the arts sector. In one session, he invited everyone to review their present situation, to see if all was well with them – a type of personal and professional health-check. First, he asked each person to draw a well on a piece of paper. To show how much energy they had at that very moment they had to indicate a water level in the well. Was this somewhere in the middle, full to the brim or close to empty? Next, each person made a list of all those things – people, activities, experiences – that top up their energy well, and then they wrote down all the stuff that drained them of energy. As a quick snapshot of our current state, this exercise is most illuminating. It was certainly an eye opener for many of the participants and also showed them that different things energise or drain different people.

Exercise:

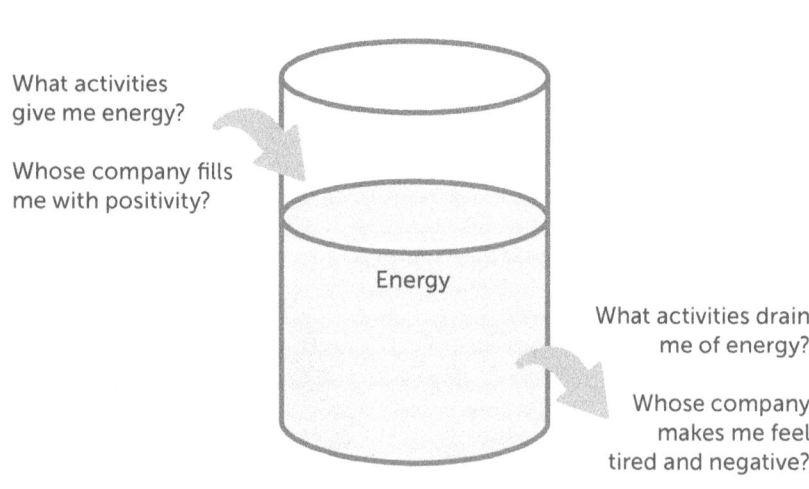

What to do and what not to do

At first this may seem like a deceptively simple exercise but it involves some deep thinking. I have used it many times to help people identify what doesn't work in their lives and also to learn what will help them to move forward. It helps us to decide what to stop doing and which situations and people to avoid. This, in itself, is an important negotiation with ourselves. Ask yourself for example; "What would it take for me to do less of this?" or; "What would make it ok for me to see this particular person less frequently?" or; "How might meeting in a different setting minimise the feeling of that person draining all my energy?" It's interesting that as soon as we explore the energy well and what or who drains us of energy, we just know. If we reflect on the people we surround ourselves with, we tend to know exactly who makes us feel wrung out after just an hour together and who helps us to feel good about ourselves, optimistic and even sparkling. Think about it: do you feel heavier when you have been in a certain situation or distinctly lighter? Most of us are rather good at knowing this and being honest with ourselves is an important part of deciding where to head next.

This exercise comes with a reminder that everyone is personally responsible for their own wellbeing or energy level and keeping it topped up. Others won't necessarily be able to tell where we are at or know how to help. But it is also an example of the fact that most of us know how to do this, once we make the effort to analyse our situation and discover how the surroundings affect us.

Making better decisions

Brothers, Chip and Dan Heath, write books that inspire people to make better decisions and good choices in life. They point out that as human beings we have an aptitude for making bad decisions. This has to do with how our minds work. They show how a traditional decision-making process can be full of potential pitfalls, for example:

// You get a choice – should you stay in your job or find another? Our first mistake is to 'narrow frame' – and assume that it's a matter of 'either/or'. Instead it's better to explore multiple options.

// Moving on – you analyse the choices. Unfortunately, in this we are often victims of confirmation bias – we look for things that support what we believe is right and we are neither neutral or objective. So, then we make our choice and the sheer emotional pressure of the situation means it's often the wrong choice.

As an alternative, the brothers suggest a process, which they call WRAP.

Exercise:

When you are negotiating with yourself for a change in career, have a look at your ideas for a change with these steps in mind, inspired by WRAP:

W: Widen your options

This is always a great idea in any negotiation so you have many possibilities to explore before you decide. Be curious and think with courage and imagination. Why not get help with this? Very few people can sit down and be creative on their own. Find out what is going on in your preferred field, talk to people who do interesting things, ask others to help you get ideas so you have a good range of possible ways to go.

R: Reality-check your assumptions

We all tend towards confirmation bias – when we look for things to validate our point of view which make us impervious to signs that point in a different direction. Take a close look at your options and play your own devil's advocate. Be a critic and take on the role of the sceptical bystander.

A: Attain distance before you decide

Take your time, develop options and ideas, let things mature in your own mind and those of others. To take a breath before you act can be frustrating. However, with major change it is vital to step back to allow yourself the time to think, and to hear what others have to say. It's a chance to refine your thoughts and pare away the stuff that just won't work.

P: Prepare to be wrong

No matter how much you try to figure things out, do your homework and sound others out, you are bound to make wrong decisions along the way. Allow yourself a margin for error and remember to congratulate yourself for at least having tried!

Envy

In negotiation, it is always a good idea to have a plenty of material to work with – expanding the pie before we slice it up. Negotiating with ourselves can be a frustrating either/or process. We prepare our arguments carefully, weighing up the pros and cons of both options, and try to convince ourselves that one of these is the right choice. If, on the other hand, we lay out all the alternatives however crazy some of them may seem initially, we will see many possible routes for ourselves. To free our minds and think new thoughts about our work options is not easy. So, to find inspiration, you might ask yourself:

"Who do I envy? Whose life would I like to have?, and What would have to be true for me to be like that?" You may well bristle at this initially, as envy is usually seen in pejorative terms, compounded by social media that provides easy access to the details of other people's lives. However, if we leave the edited Instagram picture out of the mix and look closer to home, we will discover people we admire who have chosen careers that we are attracted to. And we can use these thoughts to stimulate our own journey forward. So first we need to investigate why we envy these people's lives, and then look into which elements of these we aspire to achieve for ourselves.

SAME BUT DIFFERENT

Linda had worked for many years as a marketing director for the same American pharmaceutical company in their offices in Denmark. She travelled the world, using her many languages and developed campaigns for their products – it was hard work but fun. Eventually, internal office politics and changes in the organisation became so dispiriting that deep frustrations started to replace Linda's enjoyment in her job. At the same time, Linda's children had recently left home for university whilst her own parents and some of her best friends now lived in London. Over the course of many months, she looked at whether she could transfer to the UK. With a base in London she could still travel globally and use her languages, and work mainly from home. It took some time and considerable negotiation, both with herself and with others, but eventually she managed to move both herself and her work. Linda is now happy to be near her friends and ageing parents, seeing her kids as often as her work schedule allows and she particularly enjoys spending less time dealing with organisational distractions.

Job-crafting
Professor Amy Wrzesniewski and her colleagues from Yale University have introduced the concept of job-crafting, which is exactly what Linda did to change her situation. Job-crafting is about changing and improving your work life within rather than outside the structure in which you find yourself. If the thought of looking for a completely new job conjures up a frown then a good place to start is with where you are now, and then attempt to adjust your circumstances to fit you better.

Tasks, relationships and meaning

Wrzesniewski talks about three areas or filters in Job-crafting: Cognitive-crafting, Task-crafting and Relational crafting.

// **Cognitive-crafting** invites you to take a fresh look at what you do and to check if your work matches your deeper values and sense of who you are. Remind yourself about why, and in what ways, your work is valuable, and reflect on which elements have particular meaning for you.

// **Task-crafting** is about the actual work you do. The activities that fill your day and how these enable you to use your knowledge, skills and abilities to the full. Over time some of the original tasks in your job-description may have changed or disappeared altogether. Others may be taking up more time and space and there may be some new areas not mentioned at all.

// **Relational-crafting** is about the people that you work with and for. Are these the kind of people who help to top up your energy well? Or would it be more fun or invigorating working in a new team with different personalities?

Have a go at job crafting and it will start to satisfy your need for autonomy. If you begin to explore a known situation, with the benefit of still being paid, it may provide a less extreme alternative to resigning with no alternative in mind. The process of fine-tuning both the context and the content of your work will in and of itself contribute to your intrinsic motivation. I suggest that you analyse your current job carefully and think long and hard about your preferences, your values and strengths. "What motivates you and why? What more will you need to negotiate this change?" Keep in mind the three psychological needs of Autonomy, Competence and Relatedness described by Deci and Ryan. Then use these as filters in connection with the three dimensions described by Professor Wrzesniewski.

When I grow up
Ellen had worked in an advertising agency for a number of years but because of cutbacks, she decided to start her own consultancy business. She did regular jobs for clients but also became associated to a college, where she taught user research. There she discovered that many of the colleagues that she had always admired were the ones teaching organisational development. She told me; "I had always thought that when I grew up, I would work with organisational development, I just never got it together. But my former boss and all the professional people I looked up to worked in this field, so eventually I picked up the courage to ask around at the college and found a way to become a part of the faculty." When you can make a decision on how to move forward, you are better equipped to tailor-make your own version of a new career path, and choose elements that give you energy and make you happy.

TESTING, TESTING

In their brilliant book, Designing Your Life, Bill Burnett and Dave Evans use the image of a compass that needs calibration, to show how we may need to adjust the path upon which our lives have been set. When they work with people to help them design their lives, they question people's views on life and work and whether these clash with or complement each other. Like all designers, they know that the creativity we need to make interesting and relevant experiments, needs to be grounded in a purpose that really matters.

True North
When we calibrate our inner compass, we search for our true north to discover, or uncover, the basis by which we are navigating. We need help to check and see if there is synergy between what we really believe in and the way we work. We can test whether our life and work complement each other or if one drives the other. And then compare how this fits with our current needs and wishes to point us in the right direction. Ask yourself some fundamental questions about your underlying values and how you want to live and work. You can then create a prototype (or model) of the change you would like to experience. Change is terrifying for many people and the aim is to minimise that fear. Designers don't imagine and then produce a perfect new product; they develop and test all kinds of ideas. They accept that some of these will fail and they tease out, step by step, what really works.

Trying something out for size
Again Hannah, our financial executive who became an independent advisor, described that at 40 she started to think about future options:

"I'd had the children I wanted and was in the career I had always dreamt about. I'd been in the same company for years – all of this made me feel that it was the one and only place for me to be. And yet, if I wanted to test if this was really true – suspecting that it probably wasn't - I would need to go into the world and look at my career from the outside – to try many other things in a short time, to find out what I really and truly wanted to do."

So, this is exactly what she did. As an independent consultant, Hannah had the opportunity to work for many different organisations and tried her hand at both teaching and writing. After seven years, Hannah went back to work for an organisation knowing that in her dotage she would sit in her rocking chair and not regret the things that she might have done. Hannah made her decision to go back to work having made and experimented with a range of prototypes, to see what worked and what didn't. She was brimming with ideas about what she might do and was also aware that imagining a new career path and living it are two very different things.

Different routes

There are numerous ways to create space to try different routes, in a small way initially. Lone was tired of working as an IT-consultant even though she was excellent at her job. She finally made the decision to change when the stress of dealing with both difficult clients and tricky bosses caught up with her. Her worry was money and how to secure a regular income as a single parent. There were also serious problems in her wider family and the accumulated pressure eventually made her so ill that she had no option but to stop work completely.

During convalescence, Lone had the chance to buy a small online shop selling hand-knitted items. The business was very low key and she managed the sales and shipping from home. She felt content simply to be taking orders, packing up and dispatching parcels at a gentle pace. The nature of the business gave her time to recuperate and the chance to discover a different and calmer lifestyle. She was able to test out the idea of having an online shop and found a new way to make a little money. As much as she liked the independence of the work, to create a thriving business would have involved considerable stress. In time, Lone decided to close the shop and start her own business as an independent consultant. She worked with a range of different clients to tailor her services to suit her own interests better.

How to reduce the fear
If we can experiment with small steps, in parallel with other aspects of our work, it will reduce the fear of major change. If you bang your head against a wall and think; "This change will never happen – I can't afford to fail!" then make small changes that are easy to monitor to kick start the process. Ask yourself:

// What change would it feel safe for me to try out?
// How could I make this experiment small enough to accept the risk of failing?

Bruises and plasters are marks of honour rather than a testament to failure. In asking these questions you will recall how you learned to do something as a child – like the first time you jump on a bike and know that you will probably fall and graze your knee.

Go hopefully
When I talk to people about career change, and we explore how to approach small experiments and test new ideas, this always seems to bring hope. We could easily talk for hours about the problems: how

it's not possible to do what they'd like, about who gets in the way and about why particular circumstances make the change an unrealistic fantasy. It is important to look at what stops us from doing what we'd love to do. Take it seriously when you hit a block, look at it and acknowledge that it's there. However, if you stop at that point you will fail to probe more deeply. If we hide our dreams from ourselves, there is a risk that the insistent negative voices both within and around us will silence the excited, if timid, whisper of new possibilities. So, think of your ideas as an experiment that will happen in the real world. This is often the best way to shut out the naysayers inside your head.

Parallel lives

Certain things we can't change, but there's still an awful lot that we can. When we ask ourselves the question; "What would it take for me to be able to make this change?" we can pause the argument taking place in our heads and start to generate our own solutions. Take Karen, a 50-year-old journalist, who told me about her dream to open a teashop one day. However, until she felt it was the right time for this, she wanted to find a different and better organisation to work for. She also decided to volunteer in a café, run by a charity, to get experience and to keep her dream alive – experience that will eventually help her when she decides to make her definitive move.

NEGOTIATING WITH OTHERS
- using the right tools to achieve the change you wish for

When we decide to do something new with our work and career, this will most likely affect the people around us. Family and friends will listen to our ideas and will probably have an opinion of their own. If they are directly affected, they could even try to talk us out of it, particularly if the change involves an element of risk. Reactions are always coloured by people's own ideas and opinions about what constitutes a good life – they may object with the intention of helping us to do what we believe is in our best interests and the right thing. Envy and a fear of being left behind may also play a part – this can result in unsupportive behaviour and even attempts to sabotage our plans. It is likely that new ideas and plans for change will be met with some level of disagreement, however slight. Those close to us might argue strongly for why we should stick to our old job, and suggest frightening scenarios of failure and misery. If the change requires others to support us in a practical way, or if they hold a vital key to the change, they may just say no.

Disagreement makes us feel bad
Generally speaking, most people don't like to be in conflict with others. We all have different levels of tolerance for disagreement and most of us prefer to spend time with people who are more or less like ourselves for that reason. So, when someone disagrees with us and suggests an alternative approach, they may simply be resisting any kind of change. When we hear no from someone else, we may indeed be affected emotionally. If we introduce the idea of resigning from our salaried job to pursue a brand-new career or to take time out to think, those closest to us may hear; "I don't want to do what we have been doing any more. I want a different life." It's unlikely that they'll

leap up and crack open a bottle of champagne. If we are fortunate, they will listen to us and hear us out. But far more likely their immediate thoughts will be; "How will this affect me? What will it mean for our lives and our relationship?"

Discussion is not negotiation
One of the most common mistakes is that what people think of as negotiation, is not negotiation at all. We may believe that when we negotiate, we should use arguments to persuade someone who disagrees to switch to our side of the table. When someone else responds negatively to our proposal, our natural reaction is to explain why they are wrong, and why it's much better to agree and say yes. We are eager to persuade the other person of our point of view and so we paint a picture of all the great things that they will gain from changing their position and joining us on what we believe is the right side of the argument. The process in itself may be counterproductive. When we tell someone that they are wrong to object and wrong to think what they think, we will simply make them even more determined to dig in their heels and insist. To explain what we mean, and to give additional information about what we would like from others, is sensible in many ways but in itself will not necessarily help us to move forward together.

An alternative
An alternative is to negotiate. To respect their objections and to reflect on what interests the other person is trying to satisfy before we find a creative solution to benefit us both. This is real, result-driven dialogue with many possible joint solutions even if the interests we express are quite different. When I ask people whether they are good at taking an interest in others and really curious about what others think, most people will reply that of course they are. However, when

I examine with them how they actually communicate, they may find that what they perceive as a dialogue in their own minds is, in fact, a thinly veiled attempt to persuade the other person to abandon their ideas and viewpoints and agree with them. It's not easy to give up the idea of changing someone else's mind but this is at the core of negotiation: to find a solution together that will make both people right or, at least, right enough.

Protect your new ideas
I once talked to a woman who was considering a major change in her working life. She had been a teacher for two decades and now wanted to retrain as a psychologist. She thought about it for months and then broached the subject with her husband. He listened and then started to interrogate her about the soundness of the scheme. She stopped him and said that at this point her decision was both fragile and vulnerable. She needed a sympathetic ear, not probing and critical questions, as it was way too early for that. For this woman, her plans were like seedlings that needed time to take root. To protect herself and her ideas she asked for the kind of response she most needed at that time. To ask for what you need within a discussion framework is also a negotiation. Just as you need to respect the feelings of your partner and family, so you can ask for them to treat your ideas with respect in return.

Tailor-make conversations
You may have negotiated long and hard with yourself and with your inner critics but your plans may still be at an early stage and it feels too risky to share them with those closest to you. In spite of this, it is always possible to request and agree a constructive way to talk about these together. This approach may take some negotiation but to find the best way to think through your ideas and plans will make or break your attempt to change. In a way, you can put in an order for

your preferred form of communication based on where you are in the process. You might welcome a constructive and critical outside eye. Or you may need another creative brain to generate even more ideas for how to design the experiments you will need to conduct. You have a strong say in how you talk to others about your ideas but before you do this you need to be very clear in articulating your own needs.

Use negotiation technique to get others on board
Although you may have had considerable time to think about this, people around you will be lagging behind a little. It helps to involve those that hold the key to your change as early as possible and invite them to join the conversation and to offer their support in a constructive way. You can set the stage for this. Simply present your idea, without asking for an immediate reaction or approval, and then allow them time to reflect. Give them a chance to ask you questions and be prepared for the odd raised eyebrow. Then hold yourself back from the desire to deliver a long and heartfelt explanation - designed to convince everyone that this is the perfect deal. In this way, you will plant the seed of an idea and give it time to grow.

Expect disagreement
Even when others have had time to reflect and adapt to your plan, there's always a chance that they will disagree outright. Those closest to you may say no and then refuse to talk about it. It can be hard and disheartening to hear this response. Your head will be filled with a range of thoughts and interpretations of both the situation and the person who is disagreeing with you. At this stage, you may be tempted to collude with this and abandon your project. You may also feel angry and badly let down by those you need the most. However, this is not the time to despair or give up. Their no is the start of your negotiation process. Now is your opportunity to turn the no into a yes!

NEGOTIATION TECHNIQUES

Negotiating with others
This is a book about negotiating with yourself and finding out what you would like to achieve for yourself. However, it is also vital to consider how to negotiate with those around you. How will your decision to change affect them? Anticipating what others might say will influence your negotiation with yourself, as these 'voices' of others will join the conversation in your head about what to ask for but also about what it will be possible to achieve. If you have spent time examining the essence of your deepest wishes for a future you, then you will be more robust and make a bigger impact once you face the world around you.

Expecting trouble
If you imagine that the people who hold the key to your change, professionally and personally, will put up a fight or question your decision, then this will influence the conversation in your own mind about the change. The risk here is that you might pull back from jumping into something new because you know that others won't support you; there is no argument in the world that could convince them otherwise. The good news is that negotiation is not about convincing others to be as enthusiastic about change as you, rather it is about finding a way to get them on board. Knowing how to negotiate with others will give you a chance to counter the pessimistic thoughts you will have when you anticipate resistance from others. For example, when a little voice in your head says: "So and so will never agree to this…" a different voice can reply: "But I will find out what it will take for them to get on board and try to create options that will incorporate their concerns."

Negotiation technique 1: The ambitious first draft

Negotiation is all about the process and how we communicate, how much time we spend and what we do to facilitate a balanced agreement. Balance is a key word, and in order to make sure that the final result is as good as possible for both parties, we need to be both robust about our own demands and flexible in how to reach them, taking the other person's needs into consideration. So, when you start negotiating your change, be sure to begin by describing the optimal solution for you. If you start with the optimistic and ambitious version of how you would like things to be, then you have the possibility to give concessions over time, and this will make whomever you negotiate with feel included and the balance of give and take will be better. Instead of trying to whittle your proposal down and making it 'realistic', turn it around and start with the very best version of what you wish for.

Knowing when and where to stop

Finding out what your ambitious goal is can take some time and you may need someone helping you get there. Try to think of it as asking for something so ambitious on your own behalf, that it will give the other person the possibility (and the pleasure) of getting you to reduce your terms a bit, making them feel like great negotiators. What you also need to consider before you start crafting a deal with others is when and where to stop. This is your absolute minimum, the least you can and will accept. Having a clear idea of what your bottom line is, will help you navigate when the 'bargaining' begins. Perhaps your walk-away is the decision to change, no matter what. That come what may, things will have to change for the better, so keeping the status quo is not an option. This could give you the robustness to keep going until you find the best solution.

Negotiation technique 2: Make room and take your time
We all need time to reflect when presented with new ideas that will affect our lives. In time, most of us will develop a response that is rather more nuanced than our initial, sometimes negative, reaction. If we have spent serious time negotiating with ourselves about this change and have searched our soul, we will be robust in our desire to do something different. When people make decisions rooted in intrinsic, and deeply-felt motivation, then they will signal this quite clearly in conversation with others. Some of the hard work in convincing others will already have taken place if we are true to ourselves and find a way forward that we honestly want to pursue. However, it is still crucial that we give others the time to think about our proposal and to catch up. To see this shift in others can be a wonderful experience as they gradually become more positive and enthusiastic.

The ten-year plan
When I moved in with my partner and his three children many years ago, I gave up my apartment in the city and moved to the suburbs where the kids were at school. I work from home so have always appreciated living in the city with easy access to people and jobs. However, it obviously made sense to accommodate my partner's needs. He also had no desire to live in a hectic city environment. We ended up agreeing that, once the kids were older and had moved away from home, it would be time to move back to the city. Over the next 10 years I mentioned at regular intervals how much I was looking forward to living in a more central location. Although my partner knew why I was constantly reminding him of our 'deal', my reminders also showed him how important this was to me. It meant that we wouldn't need to start the discussion from scratch when the youngest had moved into her own flat. Finally, a couple of years ago, we moved and although we are

living in a very busy part of Copenhagen, my partner is enjoying the benefits of being so close to everything. And I'm overjoyed.

Negotiation technique 3: Investigate and be curious

When trying to come to an agreement with others with different perspectives, it is important to understand where they are coming from. When we let those around us know what we want and they don't like what they hear, our main task is to find out why they don't like it. Like investigative journalists, we need to uncover where the other person is coming from. It sounds simple but sometimes this is the hardest part. So, for example, if we have talked to our partner about our need to change, and they say it is a bad idea we can feel both angry, upset and disenchanted. We may as well give up – our partner will never agree to risk our joint savings on what could be a bright new yet uncertain future.

Digging for gold

These feelings make it even harder to listen and hear what others think, feel and say to us. If we make the time and effort to look behind the layers of resistance, then we stand a good chance of discovering where the other person is coming from. I suggest that you find out what they are worried about, for themselves and on your behalf. Are their concerns just another way of telling you they care? There is no need to become a psychologist but if you are able to find out where the resistance comes from, you will give yourself vital clues to the next step in the process. You will get ideas about how best to circumvent the obstacles and find out what the nature of their investment or interest is and the feelings that underlie this. The more you listen and understand, the more the other person will feel respected. It will then be easier for them to drop their defensive position, and join you in the search for a good solution.

Listen closely
A friend once told me about an unexpectedly strong rejection from her boss, when she suggested she would like to move to a different department. Her boss's explanation for her negative answer was vague. She described their discussion to me; "She (her boss) kept talking about future organisational changes, uncertain budgets and other general things, that I simply couldn't see as a direct cause for her to refuse my transfer." After many fruitless meetings where my friend tried to convince her manager that the move was both sensible and a great solution to so many problems, she gave up her efforts to make her boss see the light. Instead she became curious and asked a lot of questions in an attempt to the throw the net wider. Slowly it dawned on her that her boss was deeply dependent on her as she lacked confidence in her own knowledge of my friend's particular area of expertise. Her manager was afraid of losing her own job and didn't wish to reveal the gaps in her own experience, so she dug her heels in. Once my friend had understood this, she could start to work out how to save both herself and her boss from losing out.

Negotiation technique 4: Generate more options for yourself
When you have listened hard through many conversations to the concerns of the people around you, it is time to create a range of possible scenarios, or prototypes, as mentioned in the earlier section on design thinking. It's time to let your imagination begin to work. This is your chance to think of possible solutions to how you might get what you want, which will also convince other people fully to support you. There is much to be said for thinking of experimental models. It is easier and less frightening for others to say yes to trying something out rather than to make a wholehearted commitment to a new idea that is not their own. So, seek possible solutions and creative ideas which will help you to have a conversation with others who

are affected and who may resist. This invites them to step towards you and your position. You will find it more effective than presenting an idea and then spending hours attempting to convince them that this is the only way forward.

Inspired choices
You may even find, in this process, that you explore with others new approaches that might work, which you haven't thought of for yourself. Take Suzanne who could no longer see herself in her role as a high-achieving executive but could not see an obvious alternative. Her family responded with disbelief when she talked about a drastic change but their comments and ideas helped her to discover that her need to work with people in a different way could translate to a career in nursing. In spite of being in her late forties, she enrolled in nurse training. Suzanne may never have thought of this route by herself. She had financial concerns, of course, but nursing would give her many opportunities, something her family also cared about. In summary, the more options and possible solutions we have on the table, the easier it is to mix and match these to reach an agreement that everyone can accept.

Negotiation technique 5: Make balanced deals

This is the last phase of your negotiation with the people around you. Making a deal sounds like something we do when buying a used car or signing a big contract. However, it simply means that we agree on something where everyone can see that their needs and wishes will be met to an acceptable degree. We do it all the time when we tailor our decisions to allow for the differences people naturally have – here it is no different and even more important. In doing this you will need all the support you can get to make a career change. This is a vulnerable phase – it combines a sense of excitement and fear.

However, if your drive is powerful enough, and is accompanied by the support of those closest to you, it will carry you forward.

Out with the old, in with the new
Even though this change is about you, it's important to reflect on and discuss what's in it for those around you. This is not about hard bargaining but it's worth taking time to think through how the new situation will create a positive benefit for both your family and friends. I talked to a man recently who had left his very well-paid position because he could no longer live with what he felt were the flawed morals that dominated the field in which he worked. His children, now adults, had always been used to their father's financial help. Although they didn't vocalise this, he sensed their insecurity about a future life where they were not able to get the support they had relied on in the past. Once he had explained his reasons and set out the other things they would get from him now, they understood his decision. Firstly, he told them he would have far more time to spend with them and their children. He would have the energy and attention to help them in many other ways. And secondly, that they would have a father who was proud of what he was doing and much happier for it. This man had already decided to make a change but his children's feelings and perspective mattered – he needed to know he had their endorsement to feel happy in his decision.

Everyone on board
When you think clearly about how to make the change that will bring everyone on board, you will begin to make a deal. You may need to start in a small way, to try out something new on a voluntary basis or take time out and investigate what it is you really want from your career. You may decide to get involved with others who have done what you want to do and learn from them. Perhaps this is a long-

term project – you may need to keep working and place your dream to one side, whilst you save the money to enable you to take that leap. There will be many possible solutions to how you make your change. It helps to find shared agreements with others that will enable this to happen and that also makes room for them. Rather than looking for their complete and enthusiastic commitment at the very start, ask them to accept the change – this is going to happen - and invite them to have their say as to how it will come about. If you get a strong no and just ask why not, you may face multiple reasons and excuses for why this can't go ahead. So instead, try to generate both inspiration and energy by seeking their response to the all-important question; "What will it take for you to say yes?"

QUESTIONS TO ASK YOURSELF
Choose the ones you find relevant

- // How can you take time out and make space to investigate what you really want from your career? Start with a couple of hours? Or schedule some time away?

- // Who has a career and working life you envy? What is it they do, that you would also like for yourself? What would have to be true for you to be like that?

- // Do your views on life and work clash with or complement each other? How do you experience this?

- // How can you make space and time for the activities and people, who give you a boost?

- // What is the image of you in a future, and happier, work situation you can navigate by? Make a drawing. Write a 'diary entry' describing what you do and how it feels to be there.

- // What change would it feel safe for you to try out? How could you make this experiment small enough to risk failing?

- // Who can inspire and help you think creatively about possible experiments? Support you along the way?

- // What would be the ultimate version of the change, you dream of? When you think of your proposed change, describe the very best version of your idea – the most ambitious one, where you will get the ultimate result. This is the version you present to the world and start working to get your surroundings to buy in on.

- // Think about what would be the least you can accept as a result of this process of change? Remember this when you negotiate with others to prevent you from giving up or giving in too soon.

// Does the change involve an element of risk, so people around you might say no? Prepare a range of questions you can ask those, who have doubts:
   > What are your thoughts about my change?
   > How would it affect you and your life?
   > What are you most worried about?
   > I need to make a change, what will it take for you to support me in this?

// What can I do to make it easier for you to accept this change?

// Avoid asking "why not?" if you get a strong no from others. Ask instead: What will it take for you to say yes?

// Consider if other people's resistance is another way of letting you know they care?

// How might the new situation create positive benefits for your surroundings as well?

// How can you 'plant seeds' in the minds of those around you, who need to get on board? Tell others what your plans for change are, and leave them some time to think about it and getting used to the idea.

// How can you tailor-make a great solution and accommodate as many of yours and others' needs as possible? Spend time brainstorming with yourself and others about possible ways to move forward.

// How can you use 'trading' one thing for another in your negotiation with others about your change? What can you give and what would you like in return?

AFTERWORD

Guts
At a party, I talked to a woman who had quit a stressful job in the public sector to take some time out and think about her next move. When she told a male colleague about her plans for leaving, he asked her if she had another job waiting in the wings. She didn't and this was an important point for her; she really wanted the chance to find out for herself where to go from here. Her colleague looked at her and said: "Come on! If you have the guts to do that, how will that make me look!" meaning that he as a man should have had the courage to do this but hadn't, making him look weak in comparison with her. He was right in that it takes guts to make serious changes in your career when you are midlife. But he is completely wrong when he assumed that the courage to take the leap into an unknown future without a serious safety net is only for brave men who thrive when taking risks and forging new paths.

Men holding back
A male acquaintance offered his theory on why men rarely make these radical shifts in their careers, especially if that means starting over in a new field or going from a high-powered environment to something less prestigious. He was convinced that the loss of power and influence, and not least the loss of respect, is enough to keep a lot of men from considering dropping out of a career that no longer satisfies them. Just as women sometimes face unhelpful stereotyping, so do men. As a man, deciding to change from a career others may think of as respectable or high-powered, to starting over doing something completely different, or simply moving away from a profession that has defined them for a long time, could be met with a great deal of incredulity and deep skepticism.

Negotiating with ghosts
If we know, or suspect, that our desire to change our work life will create ripples in our worlds, and some reactions will challenge us, then this knowledge will almost certainly influence our decision. These ghostly voices echoing in our minds will tell us to stick to what we know and do not rock the boat, especially not at our age. These voices should be called out. They need to be examined so we can see how much truth there is in what they say. We need to do this before we experience symptoms of stress, before our relationships suffer because we are unhappy, before our health seriously hinders a change, and in enough time to enable us to actually enjoy 'the rest of our lives' at work.

Changing the way people live and work
In their book 'The 100 year life' two professors from London Business School, Lynda Gratton and Andrew Scott, spell out how our increasing life expectancy will force us all to rethink how we live and work. Not in a 100 years, but right now. We need to leave behind the traditional structure of a three-stage life of education-work-retirement and start thinking much more creatively about how we organise both our work and social lives. The urgency of changing these outdated structures have to do with our personal finances and how to earn enough to live well for so much longer. It also has to do with the need to constantly update our knowledge and skills, keeping up with the broader changes in the world around us and all the new demands of the labour market. These new circumstances will make it even more important to be able to negotiate with those you live and work with, in order to become as flexible as possible. We will need what they call 'transformational skills':
'Making the most of a long and multi stage life means taking transitions in your stride. Being flexible, acquiring new knowledge,

exploring new ways of thinking, seeing the world from a different perspective, coming to terms with changes in power, letting go of old associates and building new networks.' (P 9)

This list of helpful skills actually describes how a successful negotiator works. Changing your career and your work life is a negotiation. With yourself and others.

My mother
My mother has always been a creative woman. As a teacher at a teacher training college, she spent many years working with students to explore how they might use different ways to work with children in arts and crafts. However, her own art, primarily painting, did not get her full attention. Three daughters, a full-time though interesting and fulfilling job, and a house to run – all this left her with little room for herself. In her late forties, she decided to make a drastic change and take six months leave from the college to enroll on a painting course at an art academy in another city. My parents had always been good at talking things through and as my father shared her interest in art and also wanted to support her dream, they managed to find a solution.

Careful planning
My mum is a very careful person and unlikely to throw caution to the wind. When she first had the idea to pursue her passion, she spent a long time working out how to make it possible. Unpaid leave gave her a chance to try this out in real life and it took her out of her usual surroundings and the daily grind. The academy was a train journey away, so she rented a cheap room with a small stove in the corner and spent her days at the school. At weekends, she went home and although my dad missed her, he fully supported her project. She was

able to try things out and immerse herself in her art, and this gave her the definitive push she needed to give up her job at the age of 55 and become a painter. Before she took the final leap, my parents worked out how their savings and her early retirement bonus could cover their basic expenses. It took a while to organise things but eventually her art blossomed, and she started to make serious money from the sale of her paintings.

Still at it
She never looked back and now, at 81, she still works almost every day. She walks to her studio and spends hours listening to classical music and creating works of art that continue to sell. My mother can't not paint. If she stops, she feels very frustrated – this affects her both mentally and physically. So, in many ways her work keeps her going. It has a deep meaning for her and knowing that it is appreciated by others is an important part of the picture as well. Her next stop is a trip to Marrakech with her fellow painters from the studio.

My parents have both been a great inspiration to me and my mother has always been an example of how our inner drive can give us the strength to change, and how that change can bring benefits we didn't even dream of. Sharing our experiences of how to make changes for the better and telling stories about the detours, the setbacks, the lucky punches and the victories we encounter along the way will hopefully inspire and encourage those, that have made a first tentative step in a new direction.

COMMENTED READING LIST

**Being Wrong – Adventures in the Margin of Error
by Kathryn Schulz (HarperCollins Publishers, 2011)**
One of my all-time favourite books. Kathryn Schulz takes us through an in-depth analysis of how easily we err as human beings and why it is so hard to admit that we do. The book is a defense of being wrong, of stepping into unknown territory and examining with a critical eye what we are convinced is right, because only then will we broaden our minds and world-view and be able to accept and respect others, who are different from us. The book made me cry and laugh and feel very human – a really important book for anyone negotiating with others, which basically means all of us!

**Decisive – How to make Better Choices in Life and Work
by Chip & Dan Heath (Random House Books, 2013)**
The Heath brothers have written many books and this one focuses on their method for making better decisions using WRAP: – Widen your options, Reality check your assumptions, Attain distance and Prepare to fail. They provide helpful background on why we can be our own worst enemy when we make important decisions and explain how to counteract this in a series of steps.

**Designing Your Life – Build a Life that Works for You
by Bill Burnett & Dave Evans (Chatto & Windus, 2016)**
Silicon Valley design innovators, Burnett and Evans, have written a helpful, easy to follow step-by-step book about how to (re)design your life. They urge the reader to 'think like a designer' when making plans for what they would like to be doing next in their life. This involves, for example, a look at the obstacles we might face in this process, a review of whether they are rooted in circumstances –

therefore difficult to change – or if they are anchoring problems, that can be reframed and circumvented. They employ various techniques including exercises, diaries, mapping and brainstorming so, if you enjoy following a workbook, this is a great help when thinking up and producing different prototypes (or models) of your new life.

**Drive – The Surprising Truth About What Motivates Us
by Daniel H. Pink (Riverhead Books, 2011)**
This book has become a bestseller on motivation and is an easy and surprising read. Pink has developed his toolkit on the basis of research on human motivation and much of his thinking is based on Self-Determination Theory. The book is full of persuasive examples and cases that center on the awareness that we, as human beings, are not really motivated by money. This insight has led some companies to rethink their entire organisation; the examples are both interesting and helpful.

**The 100 year Life – Living and Working in an Age of Longevity
by Lynda Gratton & Andrew Scott (Bloomsbury Business, 2017)**
In this book, the authors unfold the huge and both positive and terrifying consequences of the fact that we all get to be so much older than past generations. Planning lives where we are healthier and live longer calls for careful thinking about finances, education, multiple careers and robust but flexible relationships. Moving from the traditional three-stage life (education-work-retirement) to multi-stage lives will have an enormous impact on all generations, and this thorough discussion of what the 100-year life might look like is hugely interesting and very relevant to us all.

The Power of a Positive No – How to say No & still get to Yes by William Ury (Hodder & Stoughton 2007)
The central message from one of constructive negotiation's founding fathers is that we often need help, when we have to say no to someone. He uses a beautiful image of a tree, which represents strong roots (what we say yes to, when we say no to something else), a straight tree trunk (being able to say a clear no) and the crown of the tree (the yes to something else, which provides a way forward). This simple drawing has appeared in almost all my negotiation classes over the years, and it hits home every time.

Women Negotiating – at work and at home by Malene Rix, 2011
In this book, I look at negotiations in both the workplace and at home, formal as well as informal and the techniques and strategies that can make the process better. The book deals particularly with how perceptions of gender affect negotiations, and what to do about the negative consequences of bias and stereotyping. The advice focuses on four phases: 1) Negotiating with yourself, 2) Influencing others, 3) The meeting and how to handle disagreement and 4) The time after the deal is struck. I also talk about the parallel negotiation, where relationships are formed and how this affects both the process and the result.

Working Identity
– Unconventional Strategies for Reinventing Your Career by Herminia Ibarra (Harvard Business Review Press, 2004)
In this insightful book by INSEAD Professor Herminia Ibarra, we discover that the path towards a new and improved working identity is a process of trial and error. Through a wide range of cases Professor Ibarra shows how there is no single answer or direct route to a new career but rather a winding road full of experiments, serious soul searching and unexpected opportunity.

OTHER RESOURCES

Jobcrafting
The work of Prof. Amy Wrzesniewski and her colleagues at Yale University has resulted in a range of interesting articles and Youtube videos. A quick search on Google will get you going.

Self Determination Theory
The work of Deci & Ryan and a great number of other interesting scholars can be accessed from the website selfdeterminationtheory.org.

Positiveacorn.com
Dr. Robert Biswas-Diener's work and thoughts can be found on positiveacorn.com

PERSONAL NOTES

www.ingramcontent.com/pod-product-compliance
Lightning Source LLC
Chambersburg PA
CBHW060206050426
42446CB00013B/3010